Searchlights for Spelling
Year 3 Pupil's Book

GU00739061

Chris Buckton   Pie Corbett

CAMBRIDGE
UNIVERSITY PRESS

A Write words to rhyme with each of these words.

cake   tail

came   train

cave   trace

Use these letters to start your words.

l   m   w   f   r   sh

B What is the most common ending when the **oa** phoneme comes at the end of a word? First, guess – is it oa, o on its own, ow or something else? Now, sort the words given.

grow   go   row

so   no   show

doe   snow   foe

flow   throw   blow

window   below   low

crow   glow   mow

sew   follow   toe

hello   woe   swallow

pillow   shallow

Spelling the *oa* phoneme				
oa	*o*	*ow*	*oe*	*ew*

C Make some word chains. Start with one of the
words below and change one letter or sound at
a time. Can you make new words, and keep the
same vowel sound? One has been started for you.

Making word chains
tray – pray – play – lay – say – stay – slay – spray – stray
low
try
bake
lame
night

Think about . . .

When you are spelling, say words slowly to yourself
and listen to the different sounds. Write each sound
down. Re-read what you have written and check it
looks all right.

A What's happening?

Change these verbs by adding ing. Put them into two lists to show what happens.

Adding ing		
	just add ing	drop e and add ing
ride		
jump		
look		
try		
make		
like		
walk		
do		
move		
meet		

B Add ing to these verbs. What happens to them? Write down what you notice.

slap	hop	smile	take
come	run	dip	write
	shop		give

Find four other words that have the same new rule for adding ing.

C These words already have ing added.
Write down the correct spelling of the words without ing.

shutting
timing   slipping
having   letting
getting
diving   amazing
clapping
naming

Think about . . .

When you are writing, stop and think when you find words where ing is added. What should happen to the spelling? Write the word down. Double-check by looking at the word after you have written it.
Does it look right?

A Sort these words into three family groups. Some end in dle, some end in ckle and all the others have a double letter before le.

dle family	ckle family	le family

middle   needle   kettle   little

candle   sizzle   noodle   buckle

bundle   chuckle

B Can you find two different patterns in these words?

Sort them into two families and give each one a title. Then find more words to add to each family.

trouble   impossible

terrible   stable

responsible   horrible

stumble   double

mumble   sensible

Sorting by le endings	

C Sort these words into three different families and give each one a title.

Sorting by *le* endings		

example   sample   vegetable   icicle

cable   uncle   able   crumple

circle   simple

Find more words to add to each family.

○ Which one is the biggest?

A Change the meaning of these sentences
by adding un or re prefixes to the underlined words.
Write out the new words.

> Tam <u>locked</u> the door.
>
> The robber <u>placed</u> the jewels.
>
> Sarah <u>tied</u> the knots in my laces.
>
> It's time to <u>visit</u> Grandad.
>
> Remi's room was very <u>tidy</u>.
>
> My new shoes are so <u>comfortable</u>.
>
> The police said the crime was <u>solved</u>.

Try writing two more sentences to show what
happened next. Use un and re words.

B Sort these words by their prefixes.

decode   deflate

unwell   unhappy

unclean   debug

Write two sentences that both include an example of each prefix.

de words	un words

Sort these words by their prefixes.

react

disagree

prefix

disappoint

disappear

prepare   predict

reappear

Sorting by prefixes		
re words	dis words	pre words

Use a dictionary to find out what the dis words mean.
What do you think the dis prefix means?

Think about . . .

When you are writing, think about whether a word has a prefix. This will help with spelling.

A Write down the opposite of these words, by adding the prefixes un or dis. The first is done for you.

tidy – untidy

well	please	obey
selfish	seen	fair
do	agree	lucky
like	kind	

Write one sentence using an un word and one sentence using a dis word.

B Rewrite this letter by changing the underlined words, so that Tom and Sam have a good time. Think about the prefixes!

Dear Mum,

Tom and I have both been very <u>unwell</u> on our holiday. <u>Unfortunately</u>, the hotel is <u>untidy</u> and the staff are <u>unfriendly</u>. This has made us both extremely <u>unhappy</u>.

This morning the manager said that he <u>disliked</u> and <u>distrusted</u> us.

We are looking forward to seeing you again.

Lots of love from

Tom and Sam

These words all use prefixes that help to create opposites. Separate the prefixes and the word roots.

word	prefix	root
nonsense	non	sense
defrost		
unseen		
displeased		
impossible		
invisible		
reappeared		

The first is done for you.

Find another word that starts with each of these prefixes.

Extra challenge

In the winter you put antifreeze in the car.
This liquid stops the water in the car from freezing.
Collect other words that start with anti. It comes
from Latin and means 'against' or 'opposite'.

A Here is a word tower that starts with s.
Can you make a taller word tower?
Start at the top and build downwards,
thinking about the next letters that
you need. You could work in pairs,
taking it in turns to write
the next letter.

Choose one of these letters to start.

    t g d r b m f p l

s

st

str

stre

strea

stream

streami

streamin

streaming

B Make as many words as you can from the letters
in the following words.

    elasticated   disobey

Make a list for each word showing words within
the word (like <u>ate</u>).

Do the same for another long word that you find
hard to spell.

C Write down words that could go in the spaces, using spelling strategies to have a go at the correct spelling.

Spiders

Some p_____ do not like spiders b_____
they trap and kill flies and other insects.

Spiders have all sorts of ways to trap their
prey. They have been k____ to leap onto their
prey, b____ trapdoors, spit out silk or even drop
a web, like a net, down onto their victims.

Most spiders are harmless, but a few can be
d_____. If you do not have antivenom,
a bite from a Red-back spider can cause d____.

Now check your spellings in a dictionary.

Think about . . .

When you are writing, use different spelling strategies to double-check the spelling of words. Make a record of any you get wrong, and find a way of remembering them.

A Make two lists, one for the five words that have an **or** phoneme in them and another for the five words that have an **er** phoneme.

or phoneme	er phoneme

The baby was born early in the morning.

I saw my jacket being torn to shreds by the bull.

Grab the sword!

The candles burned brightly.

Her new shirt got very dirty.

B

(f)
l   o
o   r   s
(t)   i   r   a
w   e   (r)   e   a
r   n   (s)   p   o   r
t   a   u   g   h   t   u
r   n   e   d   (i)   r   t   y

or phoneme	er phoneme
floor<u>s</u>	
<u>s</u>	

There are nine words in this pyramid. Start at the top.
The last letter of one word is the first letter of the next.
Write out the words. Put the **or** phoneme words in one column
and the **er** phoneme words in another. The first word is <u>floors</u>.
Arrange the ringed letters to make a tenth word.

C Sort these words into three lists:
- words with an **or** phoneme;
- words with an **er** phoneme;
- words with an **air** phoneme.

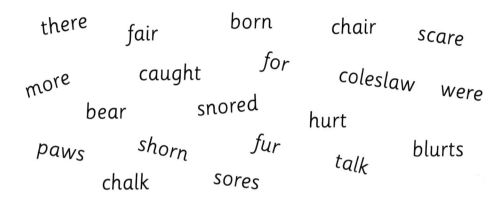

there   fair   born   chair   scare

more   caught   for   coleslaw   were

bear   snored   hurt

paws   shorn   fur   talk   blurts

chalk   sores

The words in each column will rhyme.

or phoneme	*er* phoneme	*air* phoneme

Extra challenge

Which is the most common spelling for the **er** phoneme – er, ir or ur? Make a list of as many words as possible with an **er** phoneme.

A Draw calligrams for these words.
The first one is done for you.

small — small smaller smallest
big
funny
fast
red
sad

Make up your own.

B Write boastful replies to two of these sentences.
The first one is done for you.

- I know a dog that can run fast.   Reply: Yes, but I know a dog that can run faster than the wind.

- I know a snake that is thin.
- I know a tree that is tall.
- I know a clown who is sad.
- I know a place that is hot.
- I know an icicle that is cold.
- I know a dog that is smelly.

Write out the est sentence in each pair.

- Dad is 49. Mum is 38. I am 10.
  Dad's the old____.

- John is 1m 25cm.
  Usha is 1m 22cm.
  Pete is 1m 18cm.
  Pete's the small____.

- I was annoyed.
  My sister was angry. My dad was furious.
  Dad was the angr____.

- London is 10°C. Leeds is 12°C. Dover is 18°C.
  Dover's the hot____.

- Mr Green comes at 8 o'clock.
  Mr Brown comes at 9 o'clock.
  Mr Smith comes at 12 o'clock so he's the late____.

Write two of your own, using words that end in est.

Extra challenge

Find words that change completely instead of adding
er or est, e.g. <u>bad</u> – <u>worse</u> – <u>worst</u>.
Some words use <u>more</u> and <u>most</u>, e.g. <u>more curious</u>,
<u>most curious</u>. Can you find any more?

A Put these words into two lists, one where the words just add s, and one where you have to add on es.

Making plurals	
add s	add es

bush   catch   fox   duck

dress   head   boy

map   sea   ball   toe

Can you add one new word to each list?

B Some of these words are already plurals. Some of them are not. Make a table and write out the word (singular) and its plural.

singular	plural

lip   ropes

steps   puppies

snails   horns

drums

lunch   shoe

penny

Read the poem and look out for the plurals!

The Giant's Pocket

In the giant's pocket I found
One wet hanky,
Two sweet fruit gums,
Three thick ropes,
Four spotted cows,
Five rugged rocks,

Six cool cars,
Seven long ladders,
Eight London buses,
Nine tall trees
And ten rubber tyres.

Copy the pattern of this poem to write your own number rhyme about what you might find in a giant's pocket. Use words that have different plural endings.

Extra challenge

Here are some words whose plurals do not follow these rules. Make a list of the plurals of:

- mouse
- child
- man
- foot
- tooth
- sheep
- aircraft
- deer
- woman

Use a dictionary to help you.

A Make compound words by pairing up these beginnings and endings.
How many can you make?

any	body
every	where
some	thing
no	one

Write a sentence using one of your compound words.

B Put these words together to make compound words.
Some may pair up with more than one other word.

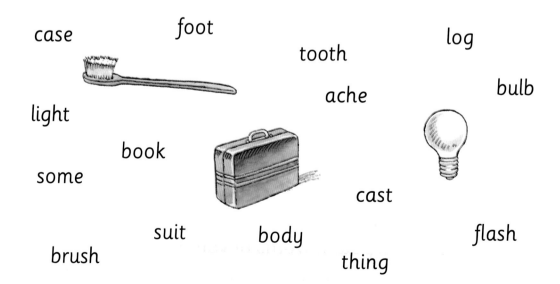

case   foot   log

                    tooth

                            ache   bulb

light

        book

some

                            cast

        suit   body   flash

    brush   thing

Write a sentence for each compound word, trying to use
the parts of the compounds separately.
The first one is done for you.

paintbrush — *She picked up the brush*
and began to paint.

footpath

seaside

gunpowder

windmill

deadline

clockwise

Extra challenge

Invent some compound words of your own.
For instance, the fridge could be called the 'coldbox'.

A Read the story.
Sort the words with silent
letters into two types.

Silent letters	
gn	kn

One day a gnome met
a knight. They became best friends and swapped
swords and knives to show their
trust. They even tied a friendship knot.
When they met a gnashing dragon their knees
knocked, but they knew they would look after
each other. It was only when the gnawing
gnat arrived that things began to change...

Can you find a silent letter word that does not start
with gn or kn?

B Insert the missing silent letters.

Mary had a little lam__. It was a crazy lam__.
It loved to __restle. She tried to stop it, but
it hurt her __rist. It loved to dive-bom__.
She tried to stop it, but it hurt her thum__.
How cou__d she ever stop it? Shou__d she
try at all? There was no ans__er.

C Read the story of the honest knight, then make lists of the words which have different silent letters – w, h, b, k or l.

Silent letters				
w	h	b	k	l

The wrinkled wrapper fell to the floor.
The honest knight put his sword
down, stopped eating his rhubarb
and picked the wrapper up.
He started to eat the crumbs, using
his thumb, which soon became numb.
He felt calm about all the folk that
he had to look after. Half of them were
family. They also had the calf, the new
born lamb and the king of the salmon.
Would they ever repay this debt? He did
not know the answer so he finished off the custard.

Extra challenge

Write a short story using as many words with silent letters as possible. Your story can't be more than 150 words long! How many words with silent letters did you fit in? Check that you've spelt the words correctly!

A Read these sentences through. Write down the words in brackets, adding the correct suffix – ly, ful or less. You may need to change some of the word endings first.

The (friend) teacher gave the children a prize.

She ran (quick) to the next lesson.

The universe is (end).

The child was (speech).

The police had been (fear).

The cowboy was (care) with his gun.

Write one for a friend to do.

B Read this passage through.
List the underlined words, changing the endings if you need to, by adding the correct suffix – ly, er, ful or less.

Slow and calm Mrs Bigger walked into the classroom. She was a kind and thought teach. Original, the class had actual behaved well. However, some children had recent been care in their work, and thought in their attitude.

Mrs Bigger dreamed <u>constant</u> of escaping and
becoming a racing car <u>drive</u>, a bank <u>manage</u>,
a pineapple <u>farm</u>, a moon <u>voyage</u>, a sausage roll
<u>bake</u> — anything other than a <u>teach</u>.

Write more lines for this poem, using the same pattern.

Slowly, the hopeful snail slithers,
Silently, the spiteful raindrop slides,
Swiftly, the beautiful swallow dives …

Extra challenge

Write a poem using this pattern.

Quickly, the fearless child swings …

A Make a list of the words with gaps.
Fill the gaps with the letters oi or oy.
Think about where the letters come
in the word. Are they at the beginning,
middle or end?

Once there was a b___ called R___
whose Dad said that he made too much n___se.
When Roy played with his t___s or dressed up as
a cowb___ he made as much n___se as ten b___s.
He was messy too. He got covered in ___l and grease.
His Mum p___nted at the mess. She had no ch___ce but
to stop him from playing. What could Roy enj___ now?

B Make a list of the words with gaps.
Fill the gaps with the letters oi, oy,
ai or ay. Think about where the letters
come in the word. You might need
to check some words with a dictionary.

Every d___ Sally liked to pl___ in the b___,
s___ling her boat or looking for fish. One d___ she
saw another boat in trouble. She stopped and w___ted.
A man was p___nting into the water. He was grasping
the boat's r___l and staring into the water.

A small t___ had fallen in and Sally had to r___se it up.
The man told Sally that he was sorry and he had not
wanted to ann___ her but the t___ meant a lot to his son!
The man gave her a few c___ns to p___ her back for
her kindness. But Sally said, 'No. I enj___ helping.'

Make up another short story about Sally using oy and oi words.

Make a list of the words that contain the **ai** phoneme.
List all the ways there are to spell this sound.

On the grey sleigh lay a plate of plain steak that no-one ate.
They had to obey orders because they hated to be late.
If the riders weigh too much the horses cannot take the strain.
It may break the sleigh and make the horses neigh.
I was late and the gauge was broken.
Today our prey has escaped.

Write a sentence that includes as many spellings of **ai** as you can.

Extra challenge

How many words can you find with the **oy** phoneme in this word square?

t	c	h	n
b	o	i	t
c	y	p	o

How many words can you find with the **ai** phoneme in this word square?

l	b	r	t
p	a	i	n
l	y	m	a

A Find the rhyming fish and write them down.
They may not be spelt in the same way!
Here is the first pair: *pair and stare*

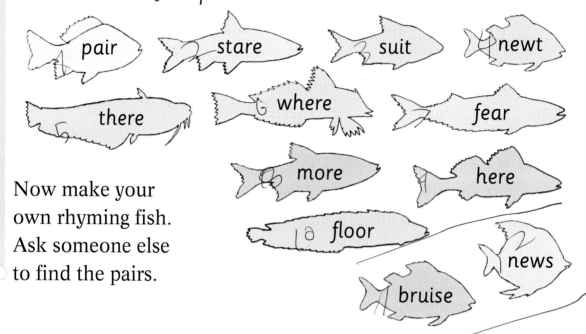

Now make your
own rhyming fish.
Ask someone else
to find the pairs.

B Continue the poem below, using rhyming words
at the ends of lines. Use some words that rhyme
but have different spellings.

I wish I was a juicy carrot.
I wish I was a pretty parrot.

I wish I was a silver moon.
I wish I was a golden spoon.

I wish I was ...

Make your own rhyming word steps like the ones below. Remember, the words must rhyme, but do not have to be spelt in the same way.

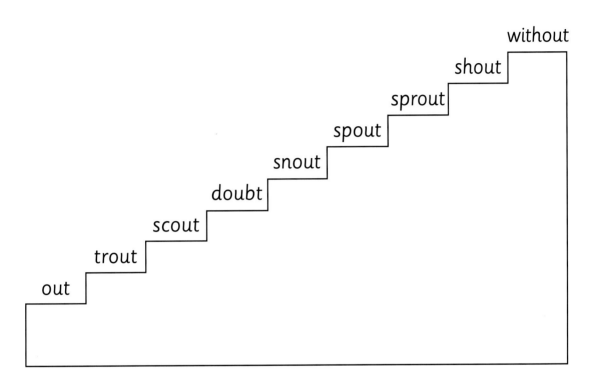

Choose at least two of these words to begin with.

oat   spot   ate   ash   own   in

Extra challenge

Who can find the most words that rhyme with <u>ball</u>? Find at least ten if you can.

A Look for smaller words within each of these words.
Make a list for each word.

otherwise   match   monkeys
whatever   another water

B Read the sentences. Look at the underlined words.
Make a list of as many words within words as you
can find (there may sometimes only be one).
The first list has been done for you.

I saw the <u>enormous</u> <u>fisherman</u> in a <u>fight</u>.

enormous
or
us

I saw the <u>rainbow</u> <u>brighten</u>
up the <u>lonely</u> wood.

I saw the <u>black</u> <u>taxi</u> <u>trundle</u> past
the <u>police</u> <u>station</u>.

C Look carefully at these words and write down a hidden word. Make a note of why this might help you remember how to spell the word. The first is done for you.

lonely — one — One person is lonely.

character
soldier
disappear
mischief
argument
happened
colour
parallel
ingredient

Extra challenge

Do you know the song Supercalifragilisticexpialidocious? Can you make up a very long word like this on your own?

A These were made by adding the prefixes mis, non, ex, co or anti. Write down the real word from each of these.

nonstick   mis-stick   co-stick

nonsense   co-sense   antisense

ex-freeze   misfreeze   antifreeze

Write sentences for two of the real words.

B Read the word riddles and write down the answers.
Add the correct prefix. Choose from mis, non, ex, co or anti.

This stops the water in your car from freezing. ___-freeze

If we do this, we will be authors together. ___-write

This type of book is about real life. ___-fiction

Something silly that doesn't make sense. ___sense

You do this when you shout out in surprise. ___claim

If you do this on the phone, you get the wrong number. ____dial

If the hands on your clock are not going the right way round, they will be going this way. _____-clockwise

Read the sentences. Write the underlined words by adding the correct prefix. Choose from mis, non, ex, co and anti.

They read the timetable and caught the wrong train.
My jeans were torn so I went to change them.
The class have to operate or they cannot succeed.
The septic will keep the cut from getting infected.
Because I hate smoke, I sat at a smoking table.
I know my tables really well because I work stop.
I would like to star with my friend in the film.
If you are ill, biotics may help to make you better.

Think about . . .

Work out the meaning of the prefixes inter and super by thinking about the meanings of these words:

intertwine   interlock   interwoven   international
superfine   superhuman   superman   supernatural

A Pair up these word roots with the correct prefix, and then make four lists. Some will pair up with more than one prefix.

side   let
root   look
hill   line
foot   stand
hand ground
side

over	up	under	out
			side

B Pair up these word roots with the correct prefix. Some word roots will pair up with more than one prefix.

Write a sentence using each word you've made. Use a dictionary to check any tricky words.

over
up
under
out

head
lift
keep
grown
arm
cover
burst
right

over + head = overhead

C By using prefixes, rewrite these embarrassing sentences that the teachers have said to the children's parents:

I am displeased that your daughter has been feeling so unwell.

It is tremendous that your son talks such nonsense all the time.

I am delighted that Shazza's handwriting is so impossible to read.

I hope Jack will misbehave himself this term.

Jon needs to view his books because he is able to do his work.

I want to tell you that Holly is a very untidy and disorganised girl.

Extra challenge

Use a dictionary to work out the meanings of:

bi   pre   photo   auto

when they are used as prefixes.

A Rewrite the words with apostrophes in their full version. The first is done for you. Make them look like sums.

I'm = I + am

you're	I've
he's	we've
I'll	you'd
she'll	we'd

Now write these words with apostrophes

cannot   had not   should not

B Some of these words have apostrophes. Write the full version of the words, without their apostrophes. Two have been done for you.

with apostrophes	without apostrophes
won't	will not
I'm	I am

I won't see you later because I'm going out. I didn't tell you before because I wasn't sure. We'll get together tomorrow, after they've had lunch. Don't worry, I can't believe she's going to be late. There isn't any time left – you'll have to go – it's half past six. Tell your brother he's got to come. I've got a present for him.

Make these sentences sound more formal
by writing the words with apostrophes in full.
The first one is done for you.

I'm riding out o' here. — *I am riding out of here.*
We weren't sleeping well when the rustlers attacked.
You'll find the cattle in the hills.
They're pretty mean.
You've been too long, Sheriff.
The cattle aren't lost.
She'll be comin' round the mountain.
I love that little ol' home o' mine.

Extra challenge

What is missing in these words or phrases?
Write them out in full. Do you know any others like this?

pick 'n' mix	Will o' the wisp
o'clock	the '60s
salt 'n' vinegar flavour	he's finished
Who's next?	Time's up!

A Join up these parts of words to make new words.
Make two columns, for two- and three-syllable words.

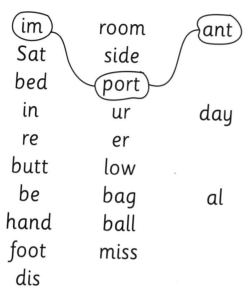

2-syllable	3-syllable

B How many syllables are there in each dinosaur's name?
Say the names to help you. Make a list and show how
many syllables each one has.

Then close your book and ask your partner to read
four names while you try to spell them. Then swap.

Triceratops Protoceratops Stegosaurus
Tyrannosaurus Iguanodon Pterodactyl
Diplodocus Brachiosaurus

Describe each of the months of the year with a word
that has the same number of syllables.
The first one is done for you.

January is disappointing

Extra challenge

The longest word in the English language is

floccinaucinihilipilification

It means 'deciding that something has little or no value'.
This is how you say it:

flok - si - nok - i - ni - hil - i - pil - i - fi - KAY - shun

(Say the part in capital letters loudest.)
How many syllables does it have?
Now try to spell it.

A Create fans for some of these prefixes.
The first is done for you.

pre

un

de

dis

re

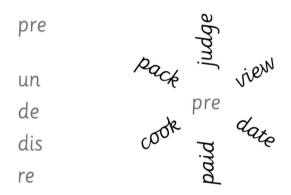

B Create fans for each suffix.
The first is done for you.

est

ly

er

y

ing

C Make some words that use a prefix and a suffix.
Try the prefixes un, im and dis and the suffixes y, ing, ed
and er. The first is done for you.

kind — *unkindness*

happy
fair
like
possible
pack
believe
polite
prove
modest
assemble
perfect

Extra challenge

Read each word. Write another word that sounds
the same but has a different spelling.

see	weather	hoarse
there	too	hear
passed	pray	

A How many words can you make?
Watch out – some of the word roots may need to change their spellings.

Word roots — cry, sing, run, tap, hope, play

Endings — er, ful, s, ing, ed

B How many words can you make from the following?

Beginnings — in, im, dis

Word roots — side, part, play, correct, patient, accurate

Endings — s, ed, ly, ing, er

How many words can you make in 10 minutes using these endings?

ear
air
are
ere
oor
ead

Extra challenge

On 20 April 1872, *Chambers' Journal* listed 61 words that can be made by using letters from the word *Cambridge*. Can you beat the record?

Useful words

Which words do you find tricky? Write them in your spelling log.
Add more tricky words to your list when you find them.
Practise **Look Say Cover Write Check**.

Key words

about	came	have	made	one	take	water
after	can't	help	make	or	than	way
again	could	her	man	our	that	were
an	did	here	many	out	their	what
another	dig	him	may	over	them	when
as	do	his	more	people	then	where
back	don't	home	much	pull	there	who
ball	door	house	must	push	these	will
be	down	how	name	put	three	with
because	first	if	new	ran	time	would
bed	from	jump	next	saw	too	your
been	girl	just	night	school	took	
boy	good	last	not	seen	tree	
brother	got	laugh	now	should	two	
but	had	little	off	sister	us	
by	half	live(ed)	old	so	very	
call(ed)	has	love	once	some	want	

ODDBODS

answer	first	lovely	out	school	when
are	girl	moment	pull	they	wood
clue	help	next	push	was	you're
even	last	our	put	water	your

44

Days of the week

Monday   Friday
Tuesday   Saturday
Wednesday   Sunday
Thursday

Months of the year

January   July
February   August
March   September
April   October
May   November
June   December

Words for maths

amount	diary	questionnaire
breadth	kilometre	relationship
circular	millilitre	row
column	negative	semi-circle
comical	positive	solution
cylindrical	prism	solve
data	problem	spherical
diagonal	product	value

Vowels

a e i o u

Consonants

b c d f g h j k l m n p q r
s t v w x y z

Words for instruction

approximate	interpret	question
decide	investigate	show
discuss	predict	sketch

Numbers

zero	twelve	sixty
one	thirteen	seventy
two	fourteen	eighty
three	fifteen	ninety
four	sixteen	hundred
five	seventeen	thousand
six	eighteen	ten thousand
seven	nineteen	half/halves
eight	twenty	quarter/quarters
nine	thirty	third/thirds
ten	forty	tenth
eleven	fifty	hundredth

Words for science

absorbent	hard	shadow
attract	iron	starches
compare	light	strong
diet	magnetic	sugars
explain	opaque	texture
feeding	repel	transparent
flexible		
growth		

Having problems spelling a word?

Try these ideas ...

- What sounds can you hear? Which letters could spell each sound?
- Think of another word that rhymes with that word.
- Break the word into syllables. (Remember, every syllable has a vowel or a y in it.) *fly* has one syllable, *fly/ing* has two, *but/ter/fly* has three
- Try different ways of spelling the word. Which one looks right?
- Think of words with the same sort of patterns, e.g. <u>true</u>, <u>blue</u>.
- Think of words with the same meanings, e.g. <u>ear</u>, <u>hear</u>, <u>heard</u>.
- Are there any prefixes or suffixes?
- Is there a rule that you know, e.g. what happens when you add ing?
- Is there a mnemonic? e.g. there is a <u>hen</u> in <u>when</u>.
- Use a dictionary or spellchecker.
- Ask a friend.
- Have a go!
- Underline the word and check it later.
- Never dodge a useful word – have your best go and keep writing!

Your spelling log

Start a spelling log. This will help you to remember the words you need to learn. These are some of the things you can put in your spelling log:

- words you often get wrong;
- ways to remember tricky words;
- things you have learned about spelling;
- words to learn for the week;
- investigations;
- word collections;
- prefixes, suffixes;
- useful spelling tips, e.g. when you add ing to a word ending in an e, drop the e, e.g. <u>move</u> – <u>moving</u>.

Learning new words

Practise **Look Say Cover Write Check**.

Look

- Look at the shape of the word.
- Make a picture of the word in your mind – take a photo of it.
- Look at the letter patterns that make up each sound.
- Break the word into syllables.
- Look for words within the words.

Say

- Say the whole word.
- Say the beginning sound.
- Say the end sound.
- Say the middle part of the word.
- Say the letter names.
- Say the whole word again.
- Over-pronounce any parts that you might forget.

Cover

- Cover the word.
- Picture the word in your mind.
- Hold it in your mind as if it's on a TV screen.

Write

- Write the word in joined writing.
- Think about the picture in your mind as you write.
- Say the letter names or the sounds.

Check

- If it isn't right yet, try again!
- Look at the tricky bits.
- Underline the tricky bits.

A few helpful hints

Adding ly

- Most words just add on ly, e.g. slow – slowly, final – finally.
- Words that end in y, change the y to an i, e.g. crazy – crazily.

Think about prefixes and suffixes when you're spelling words out

Prefixes: **un, de, dis, re, pre, mis, non, ex, co, anti**
Suffixes: **er, est, y, ly, ful, less**

Silent letters

Watch out for silent letters that might be forgotten. Make these memorable by exaggerating them, e.g. w-hen, Wed-nes-day.

Compound words

Spotting compound words can help to make spelling easier e.g. play-ground, when-ever.

Apostrophes

Remember to use an apostrophe where a letter, or letters, have been dropped, e.g. don't.

Always ...

- Silent k or g come before n, e.g. gnome, knee.
- V never comes at the end of words in English.